D0111250

In the
Company
of ANGELS

TRUE STORIES OF
ANGELIC ENCOUNTERS

Robert Strand

E/ergreen
PRESS

Mobile, Alabama

ISBN 978-1-58169-336-2

For Worldwide Distribution
Printed in the U.S.A.

Evergreen Press
P.O. Box 191540 • Mobile, AL 36619
800-367-8203
www.evergreenpress.com

Table of Contents

Introduction

The word "angel" is commonly used in our language and culture. There is the spongy-soft white "angel" food cake. Then there is an "angel" hair pasta...delicate, delectable when used with the right sauce. You can go to an aquarium to gaze at a very graceful "angel" fish. The largest western city in North America is named Los Angeles, or, The City of "Angels." One of the most spectacular and longest waterfalls in the world is "Angel" Falls found in Venezuela.

Sometimes a singer might be described as having the voice of an "angel." A peaceful, sleeping child can cause an observer to say, he or she looks like an "angel." In a world with acute needs, a person coming to offer aid is often described as an "angel" of mercy. I overheard a husband describing his wife as a perfect "angel" because she didn't have a heavenly thing to wear and is always up in the air harping about something. Someone who is physically appealing might have the face of an "angel."

This is the fourth book about angels I have been privileged to write. And I have discovered that the interest in angels is still alive and well...in fact, the more I write, the more interest is shown by readers. More people keep coming forward with their experience to share with you, the reader. My question to you is this: Have you had an angel encounter or do you know of a family member or friend who has and would be willing to share it? If so, please contact me because there are at least two more books about angels in the works. I would be delighted to include your name or if you prefer, it can still be shared on an anonymous basis.

The stories that follow are about people, just like you and

me, who have had an angelic encounter. Every effort has been made to verify original sources if a story has come out of past history. The best way to enjoy an angelic story is to take it at face value and believe in the source to have shared it in honesty. Most stories have only a personal experience...few are shared by many people. However...don't miss the first story! Seldom can a story be verified, as this one is, with pictures. This is fabulous!

An angelic story can be enjoyed by all ages. We will explore many aspects of angelic visitors. We'll look at some of the mystery, purposes, and actions of angels as they interact with our fellow human beings! Enjoy! Be thrilled! Be encouraged! And...share these with some one who needs encouragement.

Robert J. Strand
Springfield, Missouri

*To all the wonderful people who stepped out
in faith and trust in sharing their angel story.
They also shared information, opinions, thoughts,
insights, experiences and concepts in regards to angels
and their ministry among us.
Thank you…because without such help from folks
like you this book would not have
come into existence.*

Tractor From Heaven

CHAPTER 1

Angel on a Tractor

In September of 2002, DuWayne Paul took a leap of faith that opened the door for an unusual encounter with an angel half a world away.

While he was attending a men's retreat at Camp Shamineau, near Motley, Minnesota, a presentation was given about the English language camps that were held for the past ten years in Poland and Austria. (The camps have helped spur a revival among many young people in these countries.)

An announcement was made at the retreat that the Chinese government had invited Shamineau International to hold their first camp in rural China in the summer of 2003. DuWayne felt that the Holy Spirit was urging him to volunteer to go, and so he did.

In August of 2003, a group of 20 men and women set off from the U.S.A. bound for Hailar, China, near the Russian and Mongolian borders in northeast China. It was quite a journey, taking them two days to get there by planes, trains, and finally in buses (really 20-passenger vans). When they arrived, they piled into three vans along with some 40 Chinese people, children, guides and drivers.

Let's listen to DuWayne tell the story:

On the way to the camp, in a very rural part of China about 20 miles south of Hailar, we encountered a road leading to the camp that was under construction for improvements. For several weeks, all traffic on this road had been detoured through a nearby field. The problem was that it had been raining for two solid weeks, and the field was now nothing but mud and sticky, Chinese clay. Attempting to follow the tracks of previous traffic through the field, eventually all three vans became so stuck in the mud that it was impossible to go any further. We did all we could to get ourselves unstuck; the men pushing the van couldn't even begin to budge the wheels. We couldn't go forward nor could we back up; we were stuck dead in our tracks. There were no signs of life three or four miles in any direction and no farms or houses anywhere. We were completely isolated.

The American leaders gathered in the front bus to pray and ask God how to proceed. We considered walking back to the nearest village for help and then attempt to find another place where we could hold the camp.

While we were still praying, a gentleman in our group looked up and said, "We can stop praying, our answer is here!"

We opened our eyes and saw a brand new "7000 series," four-wheel drive, John Deere tractor approaching! We could hardly believe the swift answer to prayer we had just received. The driver stopped and cheerfully offered to help us. He proceeded to pull our vans out of the mud, one by one, and onto some nearby grass where we were able to get traction. He did it all with a smile on his face, and when he was finished, he abruptly left in the same direction from which he had come. We were so grateful for his help with the tractor that we formed a circle and expressed our thanks to God before we hurriedly piled back into the vans.

We watched the man on the tractor slowly drive over the crest of a small hill until he was out of our line of sight. We started our vans and followed the man over the same hill. When we came to the top, we expected to see the tractor just ahead, but the entire landscape was empty—the tractor had vanished! From the top of the hill, we could see four or five miles in every direction, but the tractor had disappeared without a trace.

When we discussed the startling events of the day, we decided that there were at least four good reasons to believe that our help was heaven sent and the man was an angel on a John Deere!

First of all, this was grasslands country, and there was no trace of farming or agriculture in the area. (From the picture at the beginning of this chapter, you can see the empty landscape.) There was no reason whatsoever for the tractor to be at this particular place.

Second, all the tractors we had seen earlier and would see in the coming days were like small garden tractors. We never saw anything approaching the 7000 series John Deere either in newness or size.

Third, take a closer look at the picture. There is no mud on the tires of the tractor! This was just not possible because of the muddy conditions of the road and the field where we were stuck.

Fourth, the kindly Chinese gentleman on the tractor refused to take any money for his efforts—very un-Chinese-like.

We came to the conclusion that we had experienced an angelic intervention. But this was not the end of the story.

We enjoyed our two weeks of conducting the English language study camp in which we taught Chinese children English, based on our American holidays—Christmas, Easter, Memorial, Fourth of July, etc. We were able to share many eternal truths during the camp.

After returning home, I received an e-mail from one of the Chinese missionaries who served as our guide. I had sent him a CD with all my digital pictures from the trip. He sent me the following astonishing e-mail:

Would you believe it? Upon magnifying the photo of the tractor that pulled your buses out of the mud in Hulun-Beier, I found that the brand name on the hood of the tractor is *Di-Er Tian-Tuo*. "Di-Er" is a transliteration for "Deere" and "Tian-Tuo" is a shortened version of "Tian-Tuo-La-ji," which literally means "Tractor From Heaven"!

There you have it: "(John) Deere Tractor From Heaven." Incredible! God was with us that day and certainly did not want us to turn back. The events of the two weeks at the camp and the impact on so many young lives would never have happened if we had turned back because of the mud. I believe to this day that we actually met an angel driving a John Deere tractor in rural northeast China!

They passed the first and second guards and came to the iron gate leading to the city. It opened for them by itself, and they went through it. When they had walked the length of one street, suddenly an angel left him (Acts 12:10).

FOOD FOR THOUGHT: What an incredible angelic encounter! How often is an intervention documented by photos and about 60 witnesses who experienced it together? You may have lots of questions about where the tractor came from and so forth, but there can be no questions about the reality of this encounter. God is still alive today, and His angelic hosts are also alive and well. Take this at face value and praise the Lord for His goodness.

"There are no mistakes, no coincidences.
All events are blessings given to us to learn from."
—*Elisabeth Kubler-Ross*

CHAPTER 2

A Heavenly Supply

During World War II, Captain Craig Johnson was leading a bomber squad in the South Pacific. They had just completed a successful bombing mission and were now returning to their base. However on this particular return flight, their plane ran out of gas, and they were forced to land on a tiny, unoccupied island that had an old abandoned air strip. Their radio was also out of order, and to say the least, their plight did not look very good.

Standing together on the tarmac in the darkness with only the moon to light their surroundings, they felt their complete isolation and began to discuss their situation. The tail gunner piped up and said, "Captain, you have often told us that the Lord would supply all our needs. Now it's time to practice what you have told us!"

The Captain told his men, "Get your emergency tents set up and go to sleep. We'll see what happens in the morning." Then, he went off alone to pray. Talk about fervent praying! His prayer went something like this: "Dear Lord, You see our situation. Without Your divine help we are all goners. Now is the time for You to honor the promise You made in Your Word. This is an opportunity to show how real You are to my men...." His praying went on for about an hour until he felt a peace descend upon him. Then he, too, crawled into a tent for rest.

In the middle of the night, one of the crew was shaken awake by a hand on his shoulder. He sat up, looked around, and saw that all the other crew members in his tent were still sleeping. He was puzzled but attempted to go back to sleep. Finding it was impossible to do, he left the tent and wandered down to the beach. Standing there and pondering what had just happened to him, he heard the rattling of barrels as the surf beat on the beach. He went to the edge of the water, and in the moonlight, he saw a raft had drifted in, containing numerous drums of aviation gasoline! He ran back to the others and hollered for them to come and help him. Half asleep they stumbled down to the beach and sure enough, they found 50 drums of aviation fuel awaiting them. They wrestled enough barrels up to their plane to fill up the tanks and took off at dawn the next morning.

As they were filling their plane, the men couldn't help but speculate where the gas had come from, but they were thankful for the rescue and relieved to be on their way back to the base.

When they returned and told their story, they discovered that a number of days earlier, a Navy ship had been torpedoed some 600 miles away. In danger of sinking, they decided to lessen the danger of explosion by placing the drums of aviation fuel on a raft and setting it loose. The raft with the 50 drums had drifted more than 600 miles, arriving just in time to be the miracle that provided their rescue!

The crew member who had been shaken awake was now positive that it had been an angel of mercy. He said, "I think an angel may have ridden on that raft until it landed on the shore, and then he came to awaken me to make the discovery."

And my God shall supply all your need according to His riches in glory by Christ Jesus (Philippians 4:19 NKJV).

FOOD FOR THOUGHT: You can easily explain away this story by thinking: "It's only coincidence." Yes, it could be, but what is behind coincidence? I choose to believe that coincidence is God at work behind the scenes wishing to remain anonymous. Well, how about you? What do you think?

"I also believe in angels because I have sensed
their presence in my life on special occasions."
—*Dr. Billy Graham*

CHAPTER 3

Do You Really
Believe in Angels?

Walt Shepard now does! Depressed over a broken relationship, he was ready to end his life. In the dark,
pre-dawn hours one Sunday, he accelerated his sports car to
more than 100 miles per hour on Interstate 10, north of New
Orleans.

Ahead, on the side of the road, he saw what appeared to
be an abandoned car. Here was his chance. He plowed into
the back of the abandoned car. There was an explosion, and
then both vehicles burst into flames.

The night manager of a nearby motel heard the crash and
called 911. Walt had been thrown through his windshield
and was lying on top of the mangled engine, trapped by the
crumpled hood. Fire raged all around him, and then he lost
consciousness.

The highway patrol arrived quickly, but the fire was so intense it kept the officers away from the wreckage. Suddenly
both the officers and the motel manager were amazed when

they saw two figures approach the car and pull Walt from the flames.

The officers wanted to interview the two strangers to find out more about the accident, but as soon as the man was loaded into an ambulance, they mysteriously disappeared. His missionary father spoke with those who had witnessed his son's rescue. They all agreed that the two unidentified figures had approached the car as if it had not been on fire. This rescue had completely baffled the highway patrol.

Walt began months of recovery with surgery and therapy. He struggled with anger, but he also began to think about his life and upbringing in the home of Presbyterian missionaries. Lying in a body cast on his hospital bed, frustrated and desperate, he finally decided to pray. He said, "Lord, I can't take it. I need your forgiveness.... Come into my life and clean me up." The next morning he woke up after the best night's rest he could remember having in the previous five years!

That day, his dad came to visit him and was overjoyed to hear about his son's prayer. His dad said, "Son, I think you were saved by two angels so you would have the opportunity to do what you did this week—get your life right with God."

At first Walt was skeptical, but now after some years have passed, he says, "I believe angels are simply part of God's natural dealings with us. It's amazing, but I believe angels rescued me from the fire that morning. And I believe they haven't stopped working."

Do you believe this story? I can't verify it because I wasn't there at this scene. But I can tell you it fits into the biblical context of what angels have done in the past, are doing in today's world, and will be doing in the future.

Are not all angels ministering spirits sent to serve those who will inherit salvation? (Hebrews 1:14).

FOOD FOR THOUGHT: Alright, let's consider the question again: Do you really believe in angels? The critics have always expressed themselves by casting doubt on things of the spiritual realm. But you have a better resource than that. The Bible, from beginning to end, simply assumes the very real existence of angels. In fact, the Bible contains more than 300 direct references to angels! Check it out for yourself in your Bible concordance.

"He has His reasons for doing what He does,
and He will explain them to us someday."
—*Emidio John Pepe*

CHAPTER 4

Angels Visit General George Washington

The following is a story written by Anthony Sherman, a close friend of George Washington:

I want to tell you an incident of Washington's life…one which no one else alive knows of except myself; and which, if you live, you will before long see verified.

From the opening of the Revolution, we experienced all phases of fortune, good and ill. The darkest period we ever had, I think, was when Washington, after several reverses, retreated to Valley Forge, where he resolved to pass the winter of 1777. Ah! I often saw the tears coursing down our dear commander's careworn cheeks, as he conversed with a confidential officer about the condition of his soldiers. You have doubtless heard the story of Washington's going to the thicket to pray. Well, he also used to pray to God in secret for aid and comfort.

One day, I remember well, the chilly winds whispered through the leafless trees. Though the sky was cloudless and sun shone brightly, he remained alone in his quarters nearly all afternoon. When he came out, I noticed that his face was a shade paler than usual, and there seemed to be something on his mind of more than ordinary importance. Returning just after dusk, he dispatched an orderly to the quarters of the officer I mentioned who was in attendance at the time.

After a preliminary conversation of about half an hour, Washington, gazing upon his companion with that strange look of dignity that he alone could command, and said to the latter: "I do not know whether it is due to the anxiety of my mind, or what, but this afternoon, as I was preparing a dispatch, something seemed to disturb me. Looking up, I beheld, standing opposite me, a singularly beautiful being. So astonished was I, for I had given strict orders not to be disturbed, that it was some moments before I found language to inquire the cause of the visit. A second, a third, and even a fourth time did I repeat my question, but received no answer from my mysterious visitor, except a slight raising of the eyes. By the time I felt strange sensations spreading through me, and I would have risen, but the riveted gaze of the being before me rendered volition impossible. I assayed once more to speak, but my tongue had become useless, as though it had become paralyzed. A new influence, mysterious, potent, irresistible, took possession. All I could do was to gaze steadily, vacantly, at my unknown visitor. Gradually the surrounding atmosphere seemed to become filled with sensations and grew luminous.

Everything about me seemed to rarefy, including the mysterious visitor.

I began to feel as one dying, or rather to experience the sensations which I have sometimes imagined accompany dissolution. I did not think, I did not reason, I did not move; all were alike impossible. I was only conscious of gazing fixedly, vacantly at my companion.

Presently I heard a voice saying, "Son of the Republic, look and learn." [Here then followed a quite lengthy vision in which he was commanded three times to "look and learn." We'll skip most of it and move to the conclusion.]

The scene instantly began to fade and dissolve and I, at last, saw nothing but the rising, curling vapor I had at first beheld. This also disappeared, and I found myself once more gazing upon the mysterious visitor, who in the same voice I had heard before said, "Son of the Republic, what you have seen is thus interpreted. Three great perils will come upon the Republic. The most fearful is the third (the help against the third peril comes in the shape of divine assistance) passing, which the whole world united shall not prevail against her. Let every child of the Republic learn to live for his God, his land and his union."

With these words the vision vanished, and I started from my seat and felt that I had seen a vision wherein had been shown me the birth, the progress and the destiny of the United States.

Such, my friends, were the words I heard from Washington's own lips and America will do well to profit by them.[1]

Gabriel, tell this man the meaning of the vision... The vision of the evenings and mornings that has been given you is true, but seal up the vision, for it concerns the distant future (Daniel 16b, 26).

FOOD FOR THOUGHT: The essence of the angelic vision and messenger to George Washington outlined the settlement and expansion of the United States as well as the Civil War. It also portrayed the dark clouds of war but indicated the United States as being victorious. I don't know about you, but this is a vision of comfort and encouragement to all Americans who consider Washington the father of our country.

[1] George Washington's Vision, Osterhus Publishing House, 4500 W. Broadway, Minneapolis, MN 55422, condensed, used with permission.

"As a statistical indication of increasing interest,
a recent Gallup Youth poll found that 76% of American
teenagers believed in angels, up from 64% in 1978."
—*James R. Lewis and Evelyn Dorothy Oliver,*
Angels A to Z

Chapter 5

Legions of Angels

Steven N. Crino, of Marshfield, Missouri, had an experience with angels that he will never forget. In the fall of 1981, his best friend's mother and his brother led him to know Christ. It was clear to Steve that they had experienced God in a way he had never known. They warned him that once a person receives Christ, he may enter into a very real spiritual war. They further explained to him that he could expect some kind of attempt to lure him back into his old lifestyle.

Let's let Steve tell it in his own words:

Shortly after I came to know Christ, I was asked to house-sit at my sister's home and care for their family dog while they vacationed. They had a large, beautiful, two-story Cape Cod styled home not far from the Atlantic Ocean. Could this be the time and place for a spiritual battle?

I worked during part of the day and also attended classes at the State Jr. College. On this particular night I was studying at the kitchen table in my sister's home. Suddenly I had a sense of terror so intense that I was afraid to even lift my gaze from my studies, convinced I would see something demonic if I did. I know of no other way to describe it than an overwhelming fear and a sense that I was in the presence of something or someone I did not care to see!

I got on the phone and tried to get ahold of my friend's mother to ask her to pray for me. She was busy, so I told my friend the situation and asked him to tell his mother so she would pray for me. As a new believer I felt she had more influence with God than I did. Still consumed with fear, I went back to my studies.

All of a sudden a peace washed over me like I had never known or even heard of before, and every trace of fear evaporated. It was instantaneous and the contrast between the way I felt just moments earlier and the peace that now consumed me was positively amazing!

Not understanding such things, I just simply lifted my gaze towards heaven and said, "I don't know what this is, but thank you, Lord!" I saw the clock on the wall reading 9:45 p.m. and made a mental note of it.

After my studies I took the dog out and when he came back in, I headed up for bed. As I walked through the dining room and up the stairs, I began to sense a heavenly presence that I will never forget. As I climbed the stairs, this sense grew more intense. As I reached the bedroom it grew more intense! With all the partying I had done in the years before, I had experienced many kinds of earthly "highs," but this experience was so far beyond that and so much better, it was like comparing heaven with hell. This peaceful presence was incredible. I could not believe that the God of all the galaxies cared enough to touch such a wretched specimen as me in this way!

I thanked God over and over again through my tears of joy. The room was filled with a glow and warmth that was indescribable. I couldn't make out distinct figures, but a general glow, a three-dimension kind of thing was present. I just knew something or someone was there.

I eventually fell into the best sleep of my life. My soul felt cleansed; my body felt renewed; my mind was refreshed. It was amazing.

The next day I called my best friend's mother and asked her if she had been praying for me. She said she had prayed that God would surround my bed with a legion of angels, and that He would allow me to feel their presence. A legion is between 3,000 and 6,000! All I know is that there was an eternal kind of happening. I then asked her about the time she had prayed, and she said that it was 9:45!

More than 20 years have come and gone since that incredible night but I have never forgotten the wonder and awe of that experience. I can hardly wait to meet the Lord and those mighty angels in heaven one day.

But you have come to Mount Zion, to the heavenly Jerusalem, the city of the living God. You have come to thousands upon thousands of angels in joyful assembly, to the church of the first born, whose names are written in heaven. You have come to God... (Hebrews 12:22-23a).

FOOD FOR THOUGHT: It doesn't seem that you must always see an angel to sense their presence. In the above illustration no angels appeared distinctively, yet this young man sensed their presence and experienced something beyond description. Perhaps you've never seen an angel, but you have known their presence!

"I believe in a loving God whose angels are
never far away. And if I let them, they will guide me
to those I should meet for His purposes."
—*Charlie W. Shedd*

CHAPTER 6

Heavenly Phone System

One Saturday night, a pastor of a church was working late in his office making some last minute preparations for the services on Sunday. It was almost 10:00 p.m. when he decided to call his wife before he left for home. He called her but she didn't answer, so he let it ring and ring and ring. He was puzzled and thought it very odd that she didn't answer. He wrapped up a few more things and then called her again.

This time she answered immediately. He asked her why she hadn't answered the phone when he called before. She replied, "The phone hasn't rung any other time this night. I've been home all night, and this is the first time it has rung." He brushed it off as a fluke and made his way home.

Two days later, the pastor was in his office again when he received a very strange call. It was from a man who wanted to know why the pastor had called him on the previous Saturday night.

The pastor said, "I don't know what you are talking about. I only made one call that night. I didn't call you, I'm sorry."

This man replied, "My phone rang and rang for about twelve rings, but I didn't answer."

The pastor suddenly realized what had happened and apologized for disturbing the man. He explained that the call had been to his wife at home that night. "Perhaps I mis-dialed and got the wrong number."

The man responded, "That's quite alright. Let me tell you my story. You see, I was planning to commit suicide on Saturday night and was ready to end my life, but before I did, I prayed, 'God, if You're up there and You don't want me to do this thing, give me a sign NOW!' At that very point my phone began to ring. And it kept on ringing until I went and looked at the caller I.D. It said, ALMIGHTY GOD, and I was afraid to pick up the phone to answer Almighty God, so I just let it ring."

The pastor then said, "The reason it showed that on your caller I.D. is that I pastor a church named 'ALMIGHTY GOD TABERNACLE'!"

The man was overwhelmed and the pastor prayed with him, and later counseled him and helped him get his life back on track.

Now, we don't know what happened that night. Did the pastor mis-dial a number that was quite different from his home number? Or did God just take that signal and send it to the man in need? Did an angel get into the phone works and re-route this signal? We don't know, but we do know that on that particular night at that particular moment, a needy man experienced a revelation of the love of God in a spectacular way with spectacular timing!

Then Nebuchadnezzar said, "Praise be to the God of Shadrach, Meshach and Abednego, who has sent his angel and rescued his servants!" (Daniel 3:28a).

FOOD FOR THOUGHT: Okay...what about you and me? As we walk our daily walk and carry out our life here in our communities, it is important to realize that our relationship with God must have first priority. And in that relationship we must also realize God really cares for each of us and knows where we are and the difficulties we may be facing. What a comfort!

"Do not forget to entertain strangers,
for by so doing some people have entertained
angels without knowing it."
—*Hebrews 13:1-2*

CHAPTER 7

An Angelic Housekeeper

Gladys Triplett scarcely had enough strength to answer the doorbell that morning in 1941 in Newberg, Oregon. Not fully recovered from the birth of their eighth child, she had spent a sleepless night and although it was only about 10:30 a.m., she was already exhausted. She felt too weak to tackle the mountain of dirty dishes, the unmade beds, and the huge pile of laundry. Rev. Triplett, her husband, was absent, being the speaker for a special meeting in another city. To Gladys, it all seemed too much to handle.

When the plainly dressed woman at the door used the word "prayer," Gladys, in her fatigue, thought she had come to be prayed for. Instead the visitor reassured her, "No, no, I did not come for prayer. The Father has sent me to minister to you, dear child, because of your distress and great need. You called with all your heart, and you asked in faith."

Then, lifting Gladys in her arms the stranger laid her on the couch and said, "Your heavenly Father heard your prayer. Sleep now, my child, for He cares for you."

When Gladys awoke refreshed three hours later, she

stared in amazement at the change in her house. All the children's belongings had been picked up and the floors were cleaned. Her baby, three months old, had been bathed and was asleep.

The dining room table, extended to its full length, was spread with the best tablecloth and set with her finest table service. She was especially surprised to see it was set for 13 people. The stranger explained, "Oh, you will be having guests soon."

Even more astounding was the appearance of the kitchen. The heaps of dirty dishes were gone; there was a freshly baked cake, a large bowl of salad, as well as other prepared food on the counter. Later, the family learned that even the cooking utensils had been washed.

Most surprising of all was what had happened to the laundry. The basket of baby clothes, a full hamper of family laundry, and all the bedding had been washed, dried, ironed and put away. The guest was just folding up the ironing board.

How could all this be accomplished? The washing machine could not possibly have put out that many loads in three hours. Furthermore, there was no dryer and it was raining outside, but nevertheless, the clothes were dried.

Gladys knew that three basketfuls of ironing usually took her almost two days to complete, yet the visitor had done it, along with everything else, all in one morning. Later, Gladys discovered that every bed had been changed and made, and each child's clothing folded and put in the proper drawer.

When the children came home from school, they noticed something unusual about their visitor. Puzzled, some of the younger ones whispered, "Who is she, Mama? She looks kind of different."

Gladys explained, "This is a wonderful friend God sent to help me today."

Gladys suddenly realized that her fatigue was gone, her body completely healed, and she felt stronger than she had in years! She attempted to learn more about this friendly helper who would simply say, "Just say I am a friend or child of God who came because of your prayer."

Shortly after the kids got home, Rev. Triplett unexpectedly returned. The meetings had been interrupted because of a death at the host church. With him were five others: the pastor, his wife, and another couple and their daughter. When they sat down to eat dinner, there were exactly 13 people at the table! The meal was the most delicious any of them could remember.

After the mysterious visitor had met Rev. Triplett and just before the family sat down at the table, she quietly slipped out.

Who was she? No human being could have done so much in so little time, have known where to put each child's clothing, or been aware of the exact number of people who would be present for dinner. The family questioned many people, neighbors, friends, even the police. No one could offer a clue as to her identity!

"I have had enough, Lord," Elijah said. "Take my life; I am no better than my ancestors." Then he lay down under the tree and fell asleep. All at once an angel touched him and said, "Get up and eat" (I Kings 19:4b-5).

FOOD FOR THOUGHT: Imagine…an angel doing housework! But, then again, why not? We usually think of them as being warriors and involved in huge projects. Why not be involved in the mundane, even in housework? It's a refreshing, perhaps new, concept of angels at work among us.

"I also believe that because He loves me, He sends His angels to bless me and to use me. Therefore, even when things seem to the contrary, I believe the universe and my life in it are unfolding as they should and everything is on schedule."

—*Charlie W. Shedd*

CHAPTER 8

Modern Manna

It was January 1964 and newlyweds John and Bonnie Eller had been serving at their first pastorate for only six weeks. At this moment they were facing a difficult financial situation. Their small church in northeast Arkansas was not able to support a full-time pastor. John had looked for employment at every business in the small town of 1,700 but had not been offered a job.

That evening Bonnie had served the last of their food supply—pancakes made with water and sweetened with their last teaspoon of sugar. "This is all we have, John," said Bonnie. "But don't worry, God called us here, and He won't let us down."

However, the young husband was understandably worried. He had never faced a situation like this before. When he went to bed, he tossed and turned for several hours. Finally, he arose, went to the living room, and turned on the light. Then he did something he would not normally recommend. Sitting on their threadbare couch, he held his Bible in his hands and let it fall open where it would. Instantly his eyes fell on a verse that stated, "God is my strength and power;

and he maketh my way perfect" (II Samuel 22:33). That settled the matter for the young pastor. He returned to bed and almost immediately fell asleep.

The next morning, about six o'clock, there was a loud knock at the side door of the humble, little parsonage. Hurriedly putting on his bathrobe, John opened the door.

Standing at the doorstep was a very elderly man holding two large grocery sacks in his arms. He was wearing a faded red flannel shirt and bib overalls. Thin, stooped and unshaven, he was carrying a walking cane in the crook of his arm.

"Here, preacher," he said in a hoarse and trembling voice, "you may need these."

Reaching out with both arms, John hugged the two heavy sacks together and carried them toward the little mohair chair in the living room. Placing them there, he turned around to thank his benefactor but he was gone!

Excited, the pastor ran outside and looked up and down the street. The man was nowhere in sight! John ran around the house and over to the church next door, but there was no trace of the man who had been there moments before.

Returning to the house, John found Bonnie smiling with big tears rolling down her cheeks. She had gone into the living room to examine the contents of the sacks. To her amazement, she found everything they normally would buy: two large cans of pineapple juice, sugar, flour, canned vegetables, meat, and even their favorite brand of coffee!

"See," Bonnie exclaimed, "I told you God would take care of us. He even knows what brands we like."

After breakfast John went through the town's tiny business district, describing the man who had brought the groceries and asking if anyone knew him. Everyone answered in the negative; no such man had ever been seen in their community.

During the remainder of their time as pastors in that little town, the Ellers often inquired about the man who had brought help to them in their need. They never saw or heard of him again.

Since then, the Ellers have never found themselves in such dire circumstances, but they have remained confident that the Lord who helped them that time would always supply their needs.

> *I was young and now I am old, yet I have never seen the righteous forsaken or their children begging bread* (Psalm 37:25).

FOOD FOR THOUGHT: What an exciting example of God's love, care, and provision for His own! Never too soon, never too late…but timed to the tick of a clock and the beat of a heart, God's provision will be there!

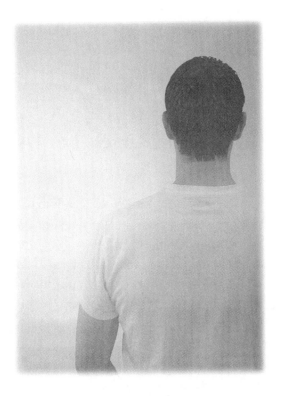

"Anyone who goes into a study of angels with
a high view of God will come away with an even higher view.
That, in fact, is the only sufficient aim in a study of angels:
that you might draw closer to God."
—*David Jeremiah*

CHAPTER 9

God Made Angels For Us

Have you ever asked yourself exactly what are angels? What kind of substance are they made of? Where do they come from? How do they get here? Why are they here? What kinds of forms do they take? How can I recognize an angel should one of them come into my life? How can I communicate with an angel? How can I know they are real? These and many more may also come to your mind. There is so much mis-information floating around today on this subject that it's a problem sorting it all out. I can't give you all the answers to these questions, but perhaps in this short chapter we can point you in a direction that will help your understanding.

But first, let's see what the angel artist, Andy Lakey, says about angels in his life:

I was four years old when my beloved grandfather tragically committed suicide. The devastation I felt was unbearable. In the midst of this time of great sadness, I realized Grandpa was in a better place.

Angels gave me a sense of comfort that put my heart at peace. Years later, in 1986, I overdosed on cocaine and knew I

39

was dying. I stumbled through the front door of my home and made it to the shower where I thought I could halt the dying process. In this impossible state of consciousness, I recall a sense of sobriety as I pleaded with God to forgive my sins and take me to heaven. I desperately vowed commitment to serve humankind if He would restore my health.

With time running out, I begged repeatedly to live, to stay in this world. I began to feel a response. A movement started at my feet. Seven beings swirled up and enveloped me, subtly recreating me. My body dematerialized as if it was lifted to another place. The images I paint now are echoes of this experience.

I awoke in the hospital; I.V.s were in my arms and my throat was sore from having my stomach pumped. How did I get there? A friend of mine, who never comes to see me, had felt the need to drop in at my house unannounced. Finding the door open, he entered and heard the shower running. He went to the bathroom and found me lying on the floor.

This was the turning point of my life. The angels were so powerful and touched me so profoundly that the impact of the experience completely changed all aspects of my existence!"[1]

Does a story like that help or raise more questions? In order to get the right answers we must begin where the Bible begins. First of all, ANGELS ARE CREATED BEINGS! God created angels. Created just like you and me. "All things were created..." (Colossians 1:16).

Then we note further that GOD CREATED THEM FOR US! God certainly didn't need angels, so He must have had us in mind when they were created. These angels are employed as a help to us humans in our needs and weaknesses.

Therefore we conclude that angels are "ministering spirits sent to serve those who will inherit salvation" (Hebrews 1:14). This is a verse we must keep coming back to for explanation.

When were they created? GOD CREATED THEM IN THE BEGINNING! God told Job that angels were already on the scene to celebrate the occasion of the earth's creation. Here's a fascinating look at the past. "Where were you (meaning Job) when I laid the earth's foundation?" (Job 38:4). Job certainly wasn't at this event, so God added more details. It was "while the morning stars sang together and all the angels shouted for joy..." (Job 38:7). It sure sounds like those created angels were having a good time, too! Job wasn't there, but the angels were!

How many angels? GOD CREATED THEM WITHOUT NUMBER! How many? We don't know and biblical numbers are sometimes a little difficult to really calculate. But how about this? "Thousands upon thousands attended him; ten thousand times ten thousand stood before him" (Daniel 7:10). There are many more references to their numbers, at least enough to provide worship in heaven as well as a guardian angel for earth's population.

ANGELS ARE HEAVENLY BEINGS! That is, all the good ones are. Heaven is their home. Jesus referred often to "angels in heaven" (Matthew 18:10; 22:30; 24:36). Heaven is their home because they belong to God, and God's home is in the heavens.

What about their substance? GOD CREATED THEM AS SPIRIT BEINGS. They are spirit beings with no permanent, material bodies. They are called "ministering spirits" (Hebrews 1:14). To be a "spirit" is to have an existence in another level; it's beyond material matter. They have no weight or dimensions.

To answer another question…ANGELS ARE POWERFUL BEINGS, BUT NOT ALL-POWERFUL AS GOD IS. Angels are limited in their knowledge, but God is not. "No one knows about that day or hour, not even the angels in heaven, nor the Son, but only the Father" (Matthew 24:36). Without God, they are impotent. They can channel the power of God through them; they operate because God allows it.

There are many more questions yet to be answered, but I trust that this has been helpful. It's a powerful biblical study which I would challenge you to undertake. With hundreds of mentions of angels in the Bible, you can research the subject until most of your questions will be answered. Go for it!

The angel (Gabriel) answered, "The Holy Spirit will come upon you, and the power of the Most High will overshadow you. So the holy one to be born will be called the Son of God. Even Elizabeth your relative is going to have a child in her old age, and she who was said to be barren is in her sixth month. FOR NOTHING IS IMPOSSIBLE WITH GOD" (Luke 1:35-36, emphasis mine).

FOOD FOR THOUGHT: Think…angel books, angel jewelry, angel web-sites, angel newsletters, angel stores, and even angel magazine cover stories. We're experiencing a phenomenon—a rising interest in angelic beings. In today's world it's easy to understand this interest. Because we live in an age of uncertainty and turmoil, it's comforting to believe

in the existence of spiritual beings who are among us to protect, help, and encourage human beings. But take the time to
sort out the myths from the truth and be assured that He still
"will give His angels charge of you, to guard you in all your
ways" (Psalm 91:10).

[1] John Lakey, Angels from A to Z, Introduction

"For he will command his angels
concerning you to guard you in all your ways;
they will lift you up in their hands,
so that you will not strike your
foot against a stone."
—*Psalm 91:11*

CHAPTER 10

Heaven's 24/7
Emergency Service

While sharing a cup of coffee with a friend, Johnny Spruill said, "You know, I am certainly glad angels don't take coffee breaks or go on vacation or sleep like we humans do. I am glad they are on 24-hour duty."

Johnny is a licensed tanker-man and owns a partnership in a business that specializes in loading and unloading petroleum products from barges in the Port of Houston. As Johnny was working one morning in 1970, the Spirit of the Lord spoke so vividly that he jumped and looked around, thinking someone had talked to him. The message was this: "Johnny, you shall walk through the valley of the shadow of death. But fear no evil, for I am with you, and My angels have charge over you."

At about ten o'clock that night, Johnny was very busy trying to unload four barges that had come into port earlier that evening. Only one other employee was available to assist him.

There was a high wind blowing, and the barges bounced

against one another and crashed and bucked in the waves. Walking on the barges and jumping from one to another was especially difficult but necessary since the unloading hoses had to be moved from barge to barge across these huge vessels.

Suddenly, just as Johnny stepped out to cross over to the next barge, a wave came up, parting the barges. Johnny fell more than 12 feet into the water and went under, deep enough to come up under one of the barges rather than between them. He tried desperately to fight back sickening fear and panic.

Just as he finally was able to surface between the barges, he remembered the strange words spoken to him that morning: "Fear no evil! Fear not!"

Johnny began to praise the Lord for help and deliverance. On either side of him were these two barges, looming in the darkness for all the world like giant steel coffins. If the wind blew again or another ship passed by in the channel, the barges would come together crushing him. He barely had room to turn sideways in the water between them.

He attempted to place his feet on either barge and climb out, but it was no use! He couldn't get a grip on the slick, wet sides of the barges, and the decks were more than 12 feet straight up. The wind continued blowing and the barges rocked! Johnny's assistant was supposed to be two barges over, working around the pump and wouldn't be able to hear anything above the noise. Johnny called out anyway, and immediately the assistant answered. He threw down a rope ladder, and Johnny quickly climbed out of the dark death trap.

For no reason that he could think of, minutes earlier the assistant had felt a hand pushing him away from his work station and so he walked over to where Johnny had been working. During this time when Johnny was between the barges, the barges remained stationary as if there were no wind or waves. The sea around them had suddenly been made calm!

Johnny said, "God's angels were on duty that night. One quieted the waves and one held the barges apart while the other summoned my assistant. We can all be glad our angels don't take coffee breaks!"

> *Last night an angel of the God whose I am and whom I serve stood beside me and said, "Do not be afraid, Paul... and God has graciously given you the lives of all who sail with you." So keep up your courage, men, for I have faith in God that it will happen just as he told me* (Acts 27:23-25).

FOOD FOR THOUGHT: It's one of the promised blessings of the believer to enjoy divine protection from accidents. Have you ever thought just how this is to happen? Psalm 91 is explicit concerning this protection from harmful accidents as the above story illustrated. This may bring to mind another question as to why we all aren't protected from disasters all the time. That's for someone wiser than me to answer, but I still take the promise of protection as a 24/7 blessing.

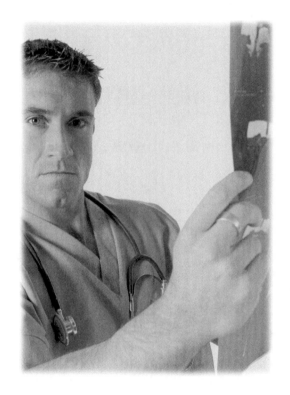

Angels where'er we go,
Attend our steps whate'er betide.
With watchful care their charge attend,
And evil turn aside.
            —*Charles Wesley*

CHAPTER 11

The Doctor Explains About Angels

In 1965 when Joel and Jane French's son Keith was two years old, he met with what could have been a very serious accident. They were packing the car for a trip, and Keith followed them in and out of the house.

Apparently, while neither of them were watching, Keith had climbed up into the car far enough to reach the gear shift and pulled the lever out of the "park" position before he slid back down to the ground. The driveway was on a slant, and the car began to slowly roll toward the street.

Let's listen to their story:

From inside the house we heard Keith's screams and came running. He was lying in the driveway, and we could see black marks from the tire tread over his left leg.

We grabbed him up and rushed him to the hospital emergency room, thanking God for sparing his life as we went. Before we reached the hospital, Keith had quit crying, and he could move his leg with no apparent pain.

After examining the x-rays, the emergency room physician just shook his head in unbelief.

Then turning to us, the doctor said, "As long as I have been practicing medicine, I have never seen anything like this. The tire marks are clearly on his leg, yet there are no broken bones, no breaks in his flesh, not even a bruise. Little boy, your guardian angel was watching over you."

When the doctor explained what had happened, it was worth every cent he charged us for it. You see, at this time, we really didn't understand at all the ministry of angels as we do now. We knew God had somehow delivered Keith, but we didn't understand what part the angels played in his protection and deliverance.

Well…the good doctor gave us the lesson in angelic help and only charged $15 for it. Well…$15 plus x-rays.

For he will command his angels concerning you to guard you in all your ways; they will lift you up in their hands, so that you will not strike your foot against a stone…" (Psalm 91:11-12).

FOOD FOR THOUGHT: None of the stories in this little book are fictional and no fictional names have been used unless there was a request for anonymity. One of the most often recurring themes when I have interviewed people is the one of angelic protection or deliverance. Right here is one of the many reasons why people find comfort in picturing a "guardian" angel who is always on duty to walk with them, shield them, protect them, keep them out of harm's way and guide them in the right direction.

"The angel of the Lord encamps
around those who fear him, and
he delivers them."
—*Psalm 34:7*

CHAPTER 12

Surviving a Plane Crash

Norman Williams tells the story of being one of the few survivors of one of the world's worst aircraft disasters. There were 653 passengers on two jumbo jets that collided on Canary Island, March 27, 1977 and 593 were killed and only 60 survived. How he escaped from this fiery crash is nothing short of a miracle.

Norm begins:

The day we left Los Angeles, my widowed mother, who has lived with me for 18 years, prayed for traveling mercies for me. As she prayed she began to weep, and this startled me because this was the first time I'd ever seen her crying like that. She was weeping so bitterly, she couldn't conclude the prayer.

At the airport, while we were waiting on the plane for our turn to take off, a KLM plane taxied by my window only to disappear into the fog. A few minutes later, our 747 slowly taxied down the same runway. The KLM jet was to taxi to the end of the runway, and then turn around and take off down the same runway. We were supposed to go part way down this runway and veer off onto a side ramp to wait for our turn to take off.

Before we arrived at the side ramp, our pilot saw the lights of the KLM in the distance. Of course, he thought these lights were stationary. And so he continued to taxi out on the runway, when suddenly, to his complete horror, he realized those lights were not stationary but were coming toward us at the full takeoff speed of approximately 200 miles per hour. He tried desperately to get our 747 off the runway, but he didn't make it.

When the jet came roaring out of the fog and saw our plane, the KLM pilot decided the only thing to do was to attempt to take off over our plane. He got the nose of his plane over us, but the landing gear didn't make it and came slicing through our jet like a hot butcher knife going through butter. Our plane was cut in half, just a few rows in front of me in the tourist section. The front part of the plane fell forward and most of the people that survived were in that section. In our center section very few people lived, and in the tail section no one survived.

Immediately on impact, thousands of gallons of jet fuel came gushing through our section like a gigantic wave. Many people were saturated with the fuel and became flaming torches just seconds later. I unfastened my seatbelt and stood up as explosions and fire engulfed the plane. To my left in the window seat was an 86-year-old woman and next to her in the center seat was her 65-year-old daughter. Immediately in front of me, in the aisle seat, was my business partner, Ted. As I stood in the aisle, I looked to see if I could help the mother and daughter. It was too late. They were on fire and obviously dead. I couldn't see Ted.

People were burning to death all around me. I could smell

their hair burning and hear their screams. The cabin was a furnace, and the thick smoke made it difficult to see and breathe. Flying debris had slashed into the flesh of the passengers, and there was the sound of crushing, grinding, exploding metal. It was hell on earth, and it all happened in a matter of seconds!

In the midst of this inferno, I could hear agonizing calls for help, mingled with loud cursing as people burned to death. It shocked me to hear cursing because I thought if people were facing death, they would automatically call on God. (From this experience, I now believe people die as they live.)

I have been a Christian since 1932 and now as the roaring flames seared those around me, portions of Scripture flashed through me mind, "I will never leave you or forsake you...I am the God that will deliver you... Fear not for I have redeemed you...When you walk through the fire I will be with you!"

I began calling aloud to God: "I stand on Your Word...I stand on Your Word!" As I repeated those five words, I saw a large chunk of debris hurtling toward me, and I put up both arms and shoved it away with supernatural strength. When I did this, I looked up for the first time since the crash and saw a large hole in the ceiling of the plane. The ceilings in 747s are more than ten feet high, but somehow I got up through that hole. The metal was razor sharp and jagged, shredding my hands. It later took 40 stitches to save my fingers that were nearly slashed off.

It's a miracle how I was able to hurl my body through the hole and over those sharp edges because when you're 52 and weigh 260 pounds, you just don't do things like that anymore. Once I cleared the hole, I fell and landed on the wing. It was difficult to keep my balance because the wing was tilted and extremely slippery with jet fuel. The engines were still running, and fire was raging in them. I knew the wing was full of fuel and that it would be only a matter of seconds before the whole thing would go because I could hear small explosions inside. I worked my way out on the wing and jumped to the ground. I'm told I fell about 30 feet. When I landed, I shattered the bones in my left foot but was able to hobble away from the plane. I heard two large explosions, and when I looked back, our entire plane was gone!

I looked down the runway 150 yards and saw the KLM exploding violently. There were 250 passengers on that plane. No one got out of it alive![1]

But now, this is what the Lord says… "Fear not, for I have redeemed you; I have summoned you by name; you are mine. When you pass through the waters, I will be with you; and when you pass through the rivers, they will not sweep over you. When you walk through the fire, you will not be burned; the flames will not set you ablaze. For I am the Lord, your God, the Holy One of Israel, your Savior…" (Isaiah 43:1-3).

FOOD FOR THOUGHT: What mysterious force could have picked up the 260 pound, 52-year-old Norman Williams and propelled him more than ten feet straight up through the top of the fuselage of that burning 747? I vote for a "travel mercies" angel who was on duty in that moment! How about you?

[1] Norman Williams, "Terror at Tenerife," VOICE, April 1979, Full Gospel Business Men's Fellowship International, Costa Mesa, California, condensed

"We are like children, who stand in need
of masters to enlighten us and direct us; God has
provided for this, by appointing his angels
to be our teachers and guides."
—*Thomas Aquinas (Summa Theologica)*

CHAPTER 13

The Travel Agent Angel

Missionary-evangelist Melvin Jorgensen faced a tough situation when his plane arrived in Belgrade, Yugoslavia. He was scheduled to be the speaker at a conference the next morning at 8:30 in the town of Subotica, about 100 miles away, but the host pastor of that church was not there to meet Melvin as he had promised.

Furthermore, Jorgensen not only didn't know the language, but also he was not feeling well. How was he to find transportation to his destination? He had no currency which would have been negotiable in Yugoslavia to buy anything, let alone a bus ticket. What was he to do?

(What Melvin didn't know was that the pastor from Subotica had already come to the airport and inquired about the missionary's flight. He was told it had already arrived, and Jorgensen was not on it. So he had decided to return home in order to reach there before dark. He, too, was in a quandary wondering what to do about the conference beginning the next day.)

Back at the airport, Jorgensen decided he should at least

get on a shuttle that would take him to the bus terminal in the city. But he wondered, What shall I do when I reach the terminal? How shall I find my way to Subotica? How shall I know which bus to take? How can I get some money with which to buy a bus ticket? How can I make myself understood?

When the shuttle pulled into the terminal, Jorgensen's anxiety increased. There seemed to be a thousand people milling about and dozens of buses coming and going. He was sick and lost.

Then a strange thing happened. As Melvin stepped off the shuttle, his attention was drawn to a man who stood there smiling at him. He was not even sure the smile was intended for him, but he smiled back.

The man was average height and appeared no different from the others, but he motioned for Jorgensen to follow him. Melvin did so because, after all, he had no other plan.

There were many ticket windows in the terminal, but which was the right one? He followed his guide until the man stopped at a window. The man talked to someone in the window, received a ticket, gave it to Jorgensen, and motioned for him to follow.

Outside was the bus-loading area. Again, which one should the missionary take? The man motioned for him to wait for his bus at an empty stall. He refused any payment and left.

The ordeal was not over. The ticket showed it was for the bus to Subotica but as time went on, no bus appeared where Jorgensen was standing. Ten, fifteen, twenty minutes passed. He began to wonder if this was the correct place to wait.

Then the special "travel agent" appeared once more,

smiled, and indicated with motions he should continue to wait. Shortly afterwards, the bus pulled into the parking stall. Jorgensen got on, showed his ticket to the driver, and they were on their way to Subotica. He arrived safely, to the relief of the host pastor, and all went well at the conference.

Now an angel of the Lord said to Philip, "Go south to the road…the desert road…that goes down from Jerusalem to Gaza." So he started out, and on his way he met an Ethiopian eunuch, an important official in charge of all the treasury of Candace, queen of the Ethiopians… (Acts 8:26-27).

FOOD FOR THOUGHT: Who was that "travel-agent" character? Why was he seemingly waiting for a complete stranger? How could he have known this missionary-evangelist needed help for directions as well as money to buy the ticket? And how did he know the man's destination was Subotica? We may hesitate to speak dogmatically and claim this special travel-agent-helper was an angel, but tell me, do you have a better explanation?

"Are not all angels ministering spirits sent
to serve those who will inherit salvation?"
—*Hebrews 1:14*

CHAPTER 14

The Mud Puddle Landing

Howard County, Indiana, Sheriff Jerry Marr received a very disturbing call one Saturday afternoon. His six-year-old grandson, Mikey, had been hit by a car while out fishing with his dad. The father and son were near a bridge by the Kokomo River Reservoir when a woman lost control of her car, slid off the embankment, and hit Mikey at about 50 mph! Sheriff Marr had seen the results of such accidents and feared the worst. When he arrived at St. Joseph Hospital, he rushed to the emergency room to find Mikey conscious and in fairly good spirits.

"Mikey, what happened?" the Sheriff asked.

"Well, Pawpaw," replied Mikey, "I was fishin' with Dad and some lady runned me over; I flew into a mud puddle and broke my fishin' pole, and I didn't get to catch no fish!"

As it turned out, the impact propelled Mikey about 200 feet, over a few low level trees and an embankment and into the middle of a mud puddle. His only injuries were to his right femur bone, which had broken in two places. Mikey had surgery to place pins in his leg; otherwise he was fine for the experience.

Since all he could talk about was his broken fishing pole, the Sheriff went to the store and bought Mikey a new one while he was in surgery so he could have it when he came out.

The next day the Sheriff sat with Mikey to keep him company in the hospital room. Mikey was enjoying his new fishing pole and talking about when he could go fishing again. When they were alone, Mikey, matter-of-factly, said, "Pawpaw, did you know Jesus is real?"

"Well," the Sheriff replied, a bit startled. "Yes, Jesus is real to all who believe in Him and love Him in their hearts."

"No," said Mikey. "I mean Jesus is REALLY real!"

"What do you mean?" asked the grandfather.

"I know He's real 'cause I saw Him," said Mikey, casting a practice lure into the trash can.

"You did?" asked the Sheriff.

"Yep," replied Mikey. "When that lady runned me over and broke my fishing pole, Jesus caught me in His arms and laid me down in the mud puddle."[1]

Daniel answered, "...My God sent his angel, and he shut the mouths of the lions. They have not hurt me, because I was found innocent in his sight..." (Daniel 6:21-22).

FOOD FOR THOUGHT: John Calvin wrote: "The angels are the dispensers and administrators of the divine beneficence toward us; they regard our safety, undertake our defense, direct our ways, and exercise a constant solicitude that no evil befall us." Now...did Mikey actually see Jesus or one of His angels? Interesting, isn't it? No matter, Mikey was spared by some miraculous intervention.

[1] *Uniting Men & Meaning*, the magazine of United Methodist Men, Vol. 5, #3, 2002

"…if you build up only a file of information about
angels or a fascination with them or even a supposed
relationship with one, but haven't encountered at least a
tug toward humble submission to the Almighty
God…you've totally missed what
angels are all about."
—*David Jeremiah*

CHAPTER 15

No Accident

It would be nice if every story were a pleasant one, but of course since we are human, that can never be.

In the late 1980s John Gordon of Springfield, Missouri, sensed the prompting of the Lord to devote more time to prayer. So, along with several others, a 4:30 a.m. prayer meeting was birthed. That meeting continued for quite a while until people began dropping out or moving away. They found themselves moving from one location to another, with each move bringing fewer people. After about three years of getting up at 4:30 a.m., John began to grow weary. Finally, he made the decision to take a small sabbatical from the meeting. To his friend Ed's credit, Ed warned him: "John, I don't think you should do this." But his mind was made up; he needed a break, and he decided that someone else could carry the ball for awhile.

Let's pick this story up with John's words:

This decision turned into a slide, then a fall, to the point that I became disinterested in the important spiritual things in my life and became more interested in worldly pursuits. I do not want to imply that I was on a big sinning program or something, but I was not interested in what was important to the Lord. I thought I would get back to spiritual things later.

About six months into my new attitude, I was test-driving a small Toyota pickup truck that a friend of mine wanted to sell. The weather that day was rainy and windy. I decided to take the truck out on the four-lane highway to see how it handled, then cut back across the country by Lake Springfield before driving back home. While driving across the dam that day, I can only tell you that what happened was a supernatural experience. It was as though an invisible hand reached down and gave that truck a shove, and off I went into a spin about a 100 feet across the little dam. The truck got almost to the end of the dam when I heard a distinctive voice: "John," He said, "I'd like to talk to you for a minute."

Upon hearing His voice, I remember shouting, "Lord, help me!"

He didn't respond immediately. The truck spun until it fell off an embankment near the end of the dam. The truck was pinned against a tree and held in place with a slim branch about 30 feet above a small cliff; through the side window I could see this limb about one foot from my head. It held the driver's side door shut and was all that was holding the truck from falling over the cliff. I didn't dare move for fear of dislodging or breaking that little branch. I was scared to death that limb would break, causing the truck to flip end over end down to the ravine below. At that moment, the voice spoke clearly: "John, you have taken Me for granted. Come back to Me."

The voice did not have to say anything more—I got the message!

Just then, a couple on their way to work saw me pinned against the tree, shouted to make sure I was okay, and then called for a tow truck. I stayed pinned in the truck until it was towed to safety. But I did not soon forget what the Lord had said to me. I sure did not want to ever take Him for granted again.

Praise the Lord, you his angels, you mighty ones who do his bidding, who obey his word... (Psalm 103:20).

FOOD FOR THOUGHT: And there's another moral for us to consider from such a story. Are you attempting to run from God? Have you decided that doing your own thing is more important than being part of God's plan? Perhaps this is the place and time to do some serious thinking about this issue at hand.

"If we could perceive our angels for just a single day,
this world would never be the same again,
nor would it ever wish to be."
—*Anonymous*

CHAPTER 16

How Angels Saved a Church

Have you heard about Joyce Berg? She's the owner of the Angel Museum in Beloit, Wisconsin. This angel museum is the largest of its kind in the world.

The collection is quite extensive by anyone's standards. There are more than 7,500 angels of all shapes and sizes, and they are made from many different types of materials ranging from wood to metal to crystal and more. This collection is considered to be world class.

This museum is said to be a heavenly spot for angel lovers. And for any collector who is interested in seeing angels displayed wing to wing, it is a true mecca.

Mrs. Berg's collection of angels is displayed in a former Roman Catholic Church. Talk about a perfect place for an angel collection—angels and churches just go together.

This church was scheduled for demolition because it had stood vacant since 1988 when the parish was closed. It eventually was spared from destruction so that Mrs. Berg could have a place to house her numerous angels. She desperately needed somewhere to put her collection because storing it all had nearly run her out of house and home. So, in a very real sense, this 98-year-old church was saved by angels. Without the angels of Mrs. Berg, this church would be nothing more than a memory.

Her collection of angels has made the Guinness Book of World Records. This collection now includes angels from around the globe. It's also interesting to note that Oprah Winfrey thought so much of this museum that she donated her own personal collection of black angels to it.

Do you think I cannot call on my Father, and he will at once put at my disposal more than twelve legions of angels? (Matthew 26:52).

FOOD FOR THOUGHT: Never before in our history has there been so much interest in supernatural phenomena. The film industry has found such subjects to be sure box-office hits. But they have created much mis-information and blatant lies about these topics until many Christian believers have tended to shy away from anything supernatural. In doing so, they have ignored an area that God wants us to know about—the reality and ministry of angels.

There is a tremendous and exciting world of angelic existence, a world God has been pleased to reveal to us in the Bible, which is the only accurate source of information we need. Again, I remind you that there are more than 300 biblical references regarding angels in the pages of God's book.

"You should be certain that angels are protecting you when you go to sleep. Yea, that they are protecting you also in all your business, whether you enter or leave your home."
—*Martin Luther*

CHAPTER 17

Angels Make a Street Arrest

A burly street-hardened police officer with a clean-shaven head grabbed a tissue from a female usher to wipe his tears. Seated with family members and 1,500 law enforcement officers from many states, he mourned Joseph E. LeClaire, Jr., a fallen comrade, at Christian Life Center, Bensalem, Pennsylvania.

"God is in control of an out-of-control world," said David A. Cawston, senior pastor, comforting the mourners. "God weeps for those who hurt. Jesus died so everyone could have a relationship with God. He wants us to invite Him into our lives as a partner."

LeClaire had been gunned down near Philadelphia at 1:45 a.m. while serving an arrest warrant on a fugitive wanted for raping a 13-year-old girl. LeClaire, who was 53, died four hours later.

Law officers risk deadly confrontations on every shift, even routine traffic stops can turn into violence. When faced with deadly force, an officer has mere seconds to decide a course of action.

According to current Department of Justice statistics, assailants killed 594 law enforcement officers from 1992-2001, an average of more than one violent death a week each year. Carlos Aviles Jr. who retired in January as a detective in the NYPD Special Victims (sex crimes) unit in the Bronx viewed his years in this unit as a special ministry. Often he prayed for and with rape victims as well as some criminals and often shared helpful literature with them.

Aviles has experienced God's intervention on the streets, too! Alone and on duty one night, he spotted a suspicious-looking man hiding in the shadows of a doorway. The man entered a club and then left a few minutes later with a loaded shopping bag. Drawing his weapon, Aviles identified himself as a police officer and approached the man.

He was stunned when the man suddenly dropped the bag and leaned over a car with his arms behind him, ready for handcuffs. "Okay, you got me," the man said meekly.

The bag contained several pounds of marijuana. It was the easiest arrest Aviles has ever made, and he found out why when the man told the officer at the desk that he saw "seven cops with their guns out" during the arrest.

Aviles, who was alone that night, believes the man really saw angels. Referring to Psalm 91:11, he adds, "That's why I know God does encamp His angels around us."[1]

"Don't be afraid," the prophet answered. "Those who are with us are more than those who are with them." And Elisha prayed, "O Lord, open his eyes so he may see." Then the Lord opened the servant's eyes, and he looked and saw the hills full of horses and chariots of fire all around Elisha (II Kings 6:16-17).

FOOD FOR THOUGHT: Do you think we are surrounded by angelic protectors? The policeman wasn't aware of angels being present, but the criminal saw seven more beings. The servant of Elisha was afraid until his eyes were opened into the spirit realm to see horses and chariots of fire! How many horses and chariots? We don't know, but they were present. It took the Lord to open their eyes in such a way as to see the reality of supernatural protection. Have you ever prayed that your spiritual eyes would be opened?

[1] "Christianity on the Job," *CHARISMA*, October 2004, excerpted, condensed & adapted.

"The Angels are the dispensers and administrators of the
Divine beneficence toward us. They regard our safety,
undertake our defense, direct our ways, and
exercise a constant solicitude that
no evil befall us."
—*John Calvin*

CHAPTER 18

Be Prepared

J ack Tibbitts of Meadow Lakes, Texas, hadn't thought of it in terms of angels speaking to him, but God entered his life in a very real way. It happened when his children were small, and he was working as a salesman for General Electric in Dayton, Ohio. He had grown up on a farm in a rural area 30 miles from La Crosse, Wisconsin, and their church was a Presbyterian church in nearby North Bend.

Let's hear Jack's story:

One day I got the strangest feeling. It was crystal clear, as distinct as if a voice told me I was supposed to prepare to preach a sermon in the North Bend church where I had grown up and attended church. Speaking from the pulpit was one of the very last things in the world I would have felt comfortable doing, and I attempted to shove it out of my mind. But the message was repeated. I ignored it…it couldn't be possible that I was supposed to take this bold step. When the message came again, I was told to use John 15:13 as a basis for what I was supposed to teach. Now this was really odd because I had never spoken in a church before, let alone behind the pulpit! Specifically the text said, "Greater love has no man than this, that he should lay down his life for his friends." I was to speak about laying down my life in a spiritual sense. I interpreted it to mean I was supposed to witness to what Jesus Christ meant in my life.

Writing out any talk was difficult for me, but I said, "Okay, Lord," and prepared. When finished, I asked, "What should I do now, Lord?" This happened in the middle of May, and the instructions distinctively came in a clear voice to go to my parents' home in North Bend over the Memorial Day weekend. This trip entailed driving 600 miles up on Saturday and back on Monday with four children under seven years of age. This was before the days of interstate highways, and I thought my wife Helen would think I was crazy (I hadn't told her of the messages I had been getting), but she agreed we should go.

We arrived at my parents' home on Saturday evening, but I didn't have the courage to tell them the real reason why we were there. Instead I asked, "Who is preaching tomorrow at church?" My mother replied the regular pastor had been called to another church and seminary students from Dubuque Seminary were filling the pulpit. I still said nothing, and we all went to church the next morning.

As we walked in the door, an old neighbor greeted us warmly but then said, "It is too bad you came today, we may not have a minister. Our supply pastor hasn't shown up. This has never happened before."

Somehow, this didn't surprise me, but I was too shy to say, "I am all ready if you want me to preach." Instead, I thought to myself, Okay Lord, You have gotten me this far, You tell them, so I just went in and took a seat with the family.

The Elders of the church quickly met in the narthex to decide what to do, and they decided to have my mother lead the service but omit the sermon. I happened to be sitting on the aisle as my mother went up to start the service. As she passed me, she leaned over and asked if there was anything I could possibly say. I replied, "Yes, I would be glad to."

I gave the sermon I had prepared and used the notes without any trepidation and with a tremendous sense of fulfillment. I don't know if it had any impact on anyone else, but it sure was a mountain top experience for me!

God will order his angels to take good care of you (Luke 4:10 TEV)

FOOD FOR THOUGHT: Are you thinking, "But where were the angels in Jack Tibbitt's story?" He hadn't really seen any, but as he has reflected on this over the years, he's concluded that it was angels at work on God's behalf. You don't have to see angels to know that angels are at work. As you study them from the Bible, one thing stands out: angels are not looking for publicity or visibility. Apparently all they have in mind, when on a mission, is to get their job done. Often, they can be at work completely behind the scenes, but sometimes so near we can almost feel their breath (if they do have breath).

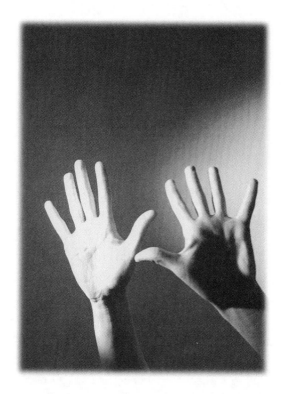

"Angels, our advocates, our brothers,
our counselors, our defenders, our enlighteners,
our friends, our guides, our helpers...."
—*Mother Teresa of Calcutta*

Chapter 19

Following Orders

Winifred Currie's favorite story comes from an experience in Belgium Congo, Zaire, when she was on an evangelistic safari with Lucille Friesen, Martha Underwood, and the nationals who were being trained in the Ndeya School.

One morning while the three women were having their private devotions, the Lord distinctly spoke to each of them the same message: They were not to go to a cotton sale as they had planned but were to specifically follow His guidance as to where to stop beside the road and follow a path into a village where God had a special person already prepared for their coming.

Let's hear Winifred's story:

Our young guide disagreed with us about traveling to the village. He said, "All the people will be working out in their fields, and no one will be at home in the village."

But Mrs. Friesen replied, "You will witness a miracle of grace today." So he reluctantly went along with us.

We followed the Lord's instruction exactly and when we

came to the village, we met an elderly lady sitting by a small fire. She had scars like raised welts on her back, which we later learned were from beatings that she had received years earlier when she had been captured by an Azande raiding party. Apparently she had remained as a slave, unable to escape, and never saw her family again.

A boy was also in the village, and when he discovered our purpose, he began beating the drum to call the people out of their fields to hear our presentation. Soon everyone gathered and the message of the Gospel of the cross of Jesus Christ in the Bangala language was given. This former slave woman's face began to light up as the name of "Yesu" (Jesus) was introduced as the name of the Son of God who had died for her sins. When we asked for those to make decisions to believe in Yesu, she began to speak excitedly in the Azande language.

She related that the night before, while asleep, she was suddenly awakened by a very bright light. Then she saw this person clothed in a white robe. She became afraid and cried out, "Who are you?" He spoke calmly and so kindly that her fear left her. He said, "Don't be afraid. Tomorrow I am sending My messengers to you, and they will tell you My name!" Then He disappeared.

She continued, "Now I know His name. It is Yesu and I want to believe in Him today!" The villagers were astonished and began to also respond to the Gospel message that day.

We had the privilege of witnessing the greatest miracle among all the miracles we had seen in our ministry in the heart of Africa. That day, everyone in the village believed in Jesus as their Savior!

I, Jesus, have sent my angel to give you this testimony for the churches... (Revelation 22:16).

FOOD FOR THOUGHT: There is no way to know how often angels have been involved in your life or mine. Maybe you have one at your side, right now, helping you turn the pages of this book. What a fantastic thought! But if they are seen or unseen, they are always on a mission that exalts our Lord and Savior Jesus Christ.

"I believe in angels—that they're always hovering
near, whispering encouragement whenever clouds appear,
protecting us from danger and showing us
the way. Performing little miracles
within our lives each day."
—*Anonymous*

CHAPTER 20

Powered by a Different Source

Gilbert O. Mort was a friend of my parents, who were entertaining him and his wife at our home in Minneapolis. I was 17 at this time in 1953, and being an avid car nut, I was fascinated by his story. The Morts had driven up in a brand new 1953 Ford, which was really something in that year for people like them and us. My dad asked about the car, and Gilbert told us the following story.

A relative who owned a car agency in the state of Washington paid them a visit. Seeing the very well-traveled dilapidated old car which showed signs of needing to be re-tired, he laughed. Then he pointed to it and said, "If you'll drive that thing out to Washington, I will give you West Coast trade-in value for it and sell you a new car at my dealer's cost. You can pick it up at the factory in Detroit."

This seemed almost too good to be true...a new car at dealer's cost and a good price for their old junker. He had a free pass on the Great Northern Railway so he could easily return home. The only problem was getting the old car out to Washington. He just knew this had to be a "God thing" without even praying about it, so he agreed. (He prayed plenty, later.)

With just enough funds to buy gas and food on the trip, he started for Washington to deliver the remains of the old car to his cousin's dealership. Two days of travel went well, and soon South Dakota, Wyoming, and Montana were behind him. He was driving on toward Coeur d'Alene, Idaho, when the gentle upgrade of Highway 10 became more than the old car could handle. The motor still ran, but the clutch was slipping so much it couldn't move, even in first gear. But along came a kindly GI who pushed him to the top of the pass.

Now it was after midnight and the old car seemed to take on new life and ran quite good downhill. In the wee hours of the morning, the miracle really happened. He was just past Spokane with only the final 100 miles left. The road was free of traffic, but snow began falling, with four to six inches accumulating. This time the motor continued to lose power, and the car was moving slower and slower until he shifted into second gear on level ground. Pretty soon, he shifted into first gear and barely crawled. The car kept going slower and slower until it seemed that every revolution of the engine might be its last. He noticed the speedometer needle was wobbling back and forth between 0 and 2 or 3 miles per hour.

Gilbert had been struggling along for several hours and should have arrived at his destination long ago, but it was still more than 50 miles away. In this discouraging situation, he began praising the Lord for His presence being with him. It was quite evident the car was dying, a foot at a time. With each turn of the engine, he moved forward a foot or so, but he continued praising the Lord. At length he was enveloped in a burst of praise and sensed God's presence in the car. Suddenly the limping vehicle began to accelerate, the speedometer needle began to climb, and he was out of the gears and into over-drive, sailing along with the praises of God rolling out of his mouth.

He arrived at his cousin's residence a little before sunup, with the motor running like new. After breakfast, he drove the car to the agency and gave the keys to his relative-dealer. He then spent the day visiting other relatives without even a thought about the ordeal of the previous night.

That evening, his cousin came home from the shop and asked Gilbert, "How in the world did you get here in that car?"

At this question, he recounted for them the whole night-marish episode and answered, "You've heard the song, 'Coming in on a Wing and a Prayer.' Well, I came in mostly on a prayer."

His cousin answered, "You can say that again!" It turned out that when the mechanics went out to drive the car into the shop, it wouldn't start. They ran the battery down and then exhausted a booster battery. Finally they lifted the hood and later showed Gilbert what they had found.

His cousin said, "When the mechanic held up the distributor, he said it was supposed to rotate, but I could see it was a mass of molten metal all melted together into one solid glob that could not move. There's no way that motor could possibly run!"

All Gilbert could answer was, "It did...you saw me start it this morning and drive it down to the shop without a problem."

"If you can?" said Jesus. "Everything is possible for him who believes." Immediately the boy's father exclaimed, "I do believe; help me overcome my unbelief!" (Mark 9:23-24)

FOOD FOR THOUGHT: A story like this defies some of the known laws of the universe. There is no normal or natural explanation for a happening like this. God intervened in a miraculous way. What other conclusion could you reach?

"Angels speak. They appear and reappear. They feel
with apt sense of emotion. While angels may become
visible by choice, our eyes are not conducted to see them
ordinarily any more than we can see the dimensions
of a nuclear field, the structure of atoms,
or the electricity that flows through
copper wiring."
—*Dr. Billy Graham*

CHAPTER 21

Chicken on the Doorknob

The following story happened to Leon Miles and his wife when they were rookie pastors in their first church whose people had all kinds of needs:

We discovered just how needy the church was when we were handed our first weekly paycheck—it was made out to us in the princely sum of $3.85. We were struck with the question of how we would be able to eat and support our little family.

Discouraged as we were and yet optimistic as beginners are about the future, we thanked the Lord for the $3.85. But we also began praying with a bit of desperation about our future and the basics of life. We decided it would be nice if we could at least eat. However, we began to believe and pray on the promises of Proverbs 3:5-6 and the promise of Matthew 6:33.

God began to prove Himself the very next day, which was a Monday. A person dropped by at 6:00 a.m. with cereal and milk for the family. At noon, meat arrived in the form of steaks to go along with the vegetables that had earlier that morning been dropped by our humble upstairs apartment.

On the following Saturday, a weekly occurrence began that lasted until the day we moved. When the doorbell rang, I shouted down the stairway, "Come on in." No response. So down the steps I went to check it out, but there was no one around. So I retraced my steps up the stairs. When I got back up to our floor in the four-unit apartment building, I saw the best fryer chicken one could buy in our town hanging on the doorknob.

For the next five years, the doorbell would ring some time every Saturday, and when we went to answer, no one would be there. It happened every single Saturday, always at different times, but without fail. It happened when we had guests or when we had none, or when we were in special meetings or just had regular Sunday services. When it rained or when it snowed or when it was nice, regular as clockwork there would be a bag hanging on the doorknob with meat inside. But we never caught a glimpse of who brought it.

Inside the bag, always wrapped in butcher paper, would be a ham, steaks, roasts, chickens, fish, etc. It was always something meeting the needs of our growing family plus any guests we were going to have that week. Who could be the angel delivering this beautiful package and how could he or she disappear so quickly?

Time passed and finally it was our last Saturday at this parish. The doorbell rang. I assumed it was the mysterious visitor, so I ran down the steps to get to the front door as quickly as possible. I caught sight of a taxi cab, with no passengers, pulling away from the curb.

We looked at the last package to discover it had come from the town's best meat market and had been sent "special delivery" by taxi. We then assumed that all the meats had come from this source. We inquired at the market, only to be told they knew nothing about the mysterious happenings. To this day we have no clue as to whom God used to provide the meats. All we know is that He did, and we were sustained. We had been fed for five years, and we never went hungry!

All at once an angel touched him and said, "Get up and eat." He looked around, and there by his head was a cake of bread baked over hot coals, and a jar of water. He ate and drank and then lay down again. The angel of the Lord came back a second time and touched him and said, "Get up and eat, for the journey is too much for you." So he got up and ate and drank. Strengthened by that food, he traveled forty days and forty nights... (I Kings 19:5b-8).

FOOD FOR THOUGHT: In a desert scene we see Elijah and we're all surprised at what he finds—a fire of hot coals, a pan of bread baking over it with a toasty, brown crust and the delicious aroma to tell him it's ready to eat! Besides that, there was a pottery jar of cool, clear water with beads of moisture running down the outside. Amazing! Where did angels learn how to bake bread? Or that humans need cool water to drink? Or that humans need sleep and rest?

"Angels don't submit to litmus tests, testify in court,
or slide under a microscope for examination. Thus, their
existence cannot be proven by the guidelines we
humans usually use. To know one, perhaps,
requires a willingness to suspend judgment,
to open ourselves to possibilities we've
only dreamed about."
—*Joan Wester Anderson*

Chapter 22

A Sudden Death Syndrome

Dick Forkner of Salem, Oregon, experienced the following story, something he will never forget:

My pastor was in the middle of his Sunday morning sermon when I felt warm and removed my jacket. It seemed as though my lungs weren't getting enough oxygen. Then a yellow sheet seemed to be pulled down in front of my eyes. The next thing I remember I was looking up into the face of a paramedic.

My wife, Evelyn, said she had touched my hand, and it was cold and damp. My head fell onto her shoulder, and I stopped breathing. She yelled for someone to call 911.

Four men laid me in the aisle and an off-duty para-medic and a nurse rushed to my side. The wife of our senior adult minister told Evelyn, "We have to wait for the ambulance, but God doesn't have to wait." Those words calmed my wife, who had seen her first husband die in her arms.

Suddenly, another figure came up the aisle, not running or walking. He just seemed to appear. He said to Evelyn, "I'm a doctor." He knelt beside me, shook his head "No!" and then hit me quite hard in the chest. At that same moment, my pastor and the entire congregation began to pray and I began to breathe.

The ambulance took me to the hospital. Later I attempted to contact those who had assisted me. When I asked about the "doctor," everyone gave the same reply, "There was no doctor." My wife and a retired minister were the only ones who had seen him. They both gave an identical account, but nobody else had seen this man.

The medical staff said I should have had heart and lung damage, but there were none. They also said the only way my heart could have been quickly started was by a hard blow to the chest. No one, except my wife and the retired minister, had seen the "doctor" give the blow to my chest. However, I did have a sore spot there the next day.

During nearly a month of testing, no reason could be found for either my sudden collapse or remarkable recovery. It was medically determined I had had "sudden death syndrome."

I know it was a messenger of God who brought me back...and it was the Lord who healed me.

My strength is gone and I can hardly breathe. Again the one who looked like a man touched me and gave me strength. "Do not be afraid, O man..." he said. "Peace! Be strong now; be strong!" (Daniel 10:17b-19)

FOOD FOR THOUGHT: Angels seem to be able to assume just about any kind of form from bright and shining beings of light to a very human form. In this situation, one appeared like a doctor and acted like a doctor. But isn't it strange that only two people saw this "doctor" in action? Here is another example of an angel at work, carrying out a single mission of mercy, with exquisite timing!

"Angels come to help and guide us in as many guises as
there are people who need their assistance. Sometimes we see
their ethereal, heavenly shadow, bright with light and
radiance. Sometimes we only feel their nearness or
hear their whisper. And sometimes they look
no different from ourselves...."
—*Eileen Elias Freeman,* Touched by Angels

CHAPTER 23

An Angel Look-Alike?

How did this stranger know his name? Burton Pierce was puzzled. This day had been one of a series of unusual happenings, and now this was the strangest of them all.

On Friday, August 15, 1969, Burt, with his wife, his mother, and a grand-niece had decided to drive from a town in Upper Michigan to Duluth, Minnesota, about 100 miles away. They took the scenic route, which bordered Lake Superior, instead of a more direct one.

After stopping for lunch, they continued driving along the Red Cliff Indian Reservation. About 2:00 p.m., after traveling a short distance past a small roadside park, Burt was strangely and strongly impressed to turn around and return to the park. His passengers questioned his strange decision, but he followed this very strong impulse.

They got out of the car and sat down at a picnic table to rest and wait. Quickly, a man emerged from another part of the park. It was evident he had been crying.

Burt tells us what happened:

He walked directly toward me and after a few seconds said, "You're Burt, aren't you?"

I didn't know how he knew my name but I was so concerned about the man that I put my curiosity aside. We sat down facing each other, and he poured out his heart. Half American Indian, Bill spilled out the tragic story of an auto accident that happened while he was driving in Oregon. His wife and only daughter had died when the car plunged into a canyon. He was so overcome with remorse and loneliness he had planned to take his own life that day.

I encouraged Bill to look to the Savior who could meet his needs. I shared some of God's Word with him. I prayed with him, and Bill opened his heart and invited Jesus Christ to come into his troubled life.

Then I realized why I had felt this strong impression to turn around and come to this remote roadside park. But one thing puzzled me, so I asked Bill, "How did you know my name?" I thought perhaps we had met before.

He looked at me strangely. "Why, don't you remember?" he asked. "We were talking this morning down in the lower park."

"But Bill," I said, "I was a long way from here this morning."

"No, Burt, it was you. It looked just like you, except you had on a different colored sport shirt. And you told me to come to the upper part of the park and wait for you."

I assured him it couldn't have been me and told him where I had been that morning, visiting my mother in Upper Michigan.

Then he looked at me and asked, "Well, where are you from?"

"I live in Springfield, Missouri," I told him.

He immediately replied, "You told me this morning that you were from Missouri!"

All of those who participated in this strange encounter later became convinced that the person Bill had met that morning must have been an angelic messenger sent to keep Bill from his plans of suicide until Burt could talk and pray with him to invite the Savior into his life. It turned out that Bill had been waiting hour after hour for God's human messenger to arrive!

During the night Paul had a vision of a man of Macedonia standing and begging him, "come over to Macedonia and help us" (Acts 16:9).

FOOD FOR THOUGHT: How about that? An angelic look-a-like! Haven't you been interested in the variety of ways, recorded in this little book, in which angelic visitors have ministered and appeared? Why shouldn't one look like another human? God is unlimited in the methods He uses to accomplish His purposes.

"Whether each of the faithful has a particular angel
assigned him for his defence, I cannot venture certainly
to affirm; not one angel only has the care of every one of
us, but that all the angels together with one
consent watch over our salvation."
—*John Calvin*

CHAPTER 24

Do We All Have
A Guardian Angel?

We'll answer that question after we first read what Lester Sumrall wrote:

Some years ago I was traveling with a group up near the border of Tibet. Somehow, I became lost...I mean absolutely lost! You know the feeling. I was separated from my party from early morning until about 4:30 that afternoon. I was in a little Chinese village, all by myself, without knowing one word of their language. I was sad, lost, tired, and almost in tears.

Then I noticed a young man come riding through the gates on a majestic horse, quite different from the mountain mules we were using. He rode right up to me, dismounted, and began to speak in perfect English.

"Where did you come from?" I asked. "How is it that you speak English so beautifully?"

He smiled and replied, "I know the party you're looking for. I met them on the road. If you go out this gate and then travel for about two hours on this path, you'll find them."

I took his advice. I got on my mule, headed out the gate, and sure enough, before too long I found the folks I had been traveling with. I inquired of them about the young man. They hadn't seen him and didn't know anything about him! I'm positive it was my guardian angel!

I cannot prove conclusively from the Bible the existence of your own personal guardian angel. However, there are some references, when taken together that seem to strongly suggest this possibility. At least, I am convinced.

Let's start with Psalm 91:11,

For He will command His angels concerning YOU to guard YOU in all YOUR ways; they will lift YOU up in their hands…(emphasis mine).

Notice that these pronouns are all singular! This goes along with the concept we have of a God who is always very much aware of our needs and concerns and is able to minister to us in our needs.

Come with me to the Old Testament where a dying Jacob was blessing his grandchildren, Joseph's sons. The setting is found in Genesis 48:15-16,

Then he blessed Joseph and said, "May the God before whom my fathers Abraham and Isaac walked, the God who has been MY shepherd all MY life to this day, the ANGEL who has delivered ME from all harm…may he bless these boys" (emphasis mine).

Was that a guardian angel who had watched over Jacob in his many adventures of his life? I like to think it was.

How close is your personal angel when you might need him? There is an answer in Psalm 34:7,

The angel of the Lord encamps around those who fear Him, and He delivers them!

It literally means your angel puts up his tent around you, if you fear the Lord. You don't have to worry about leaving him behind on your next plane trip!

Let's not overlook little children or think they are not very important in God's plans. It was Jesus himself who in Matthew 18:10 said,

See that you do not look down on one of these little ones. For I tell you that THEIR ANGELS in heaven always see the face of my Father in heaven (emphasis mine).

That's the strongest biblical suggestion that each child and by inference, each person, has a guardian angel all his or her own. Maybe it's because little kids need more angelic protection than adults.

As I looked, thrones were set in place, and the Ancient of Days took his seat. His clothing was as white as snow; the hair of his head was white like wool. His throne was flaming with fire, and its wheels were all ablaze. A river of fire was flowing, coming out from before him. THOUSANDS UPON THOUSANDS attended Him; TEN THOUSAND TIMES TEN THOUSAND stood before Him (Daniel 7:9-10 emphasis mine).

FOOD FOR THOUGHT: Perhaps you are thinking: "There are more than six billion people on this earth and that number is growing. Are there enough angels to go around?" If you believe that God has assigned a private, guardian angel to you and me, then surely, there must be more than enough angels to go around and do the job. They were created by God in the beginning and if He runs short, surely He can create more!

"The wars among nations on earth are merely
popgun affairs compared to the fierceness of the
battle in the spiritual unseen world."
—*Dr. Billy Graham*

CHAPTER 25

The Angel Customers

Today Robert owns an over-the-road trucking company, but before he got into the trucking business, he had purchased a sporting goods store. He was the lone employee in the beginning, and the store happened to be in an out-of-the-way part of town, which helped to make him feel even more isolated.

One day while expressing his concerns about his business to his pastor, the idea struck him to ask the pastor and some of the church elders to come over and pray for the protection of himself and his store. When they came, they also prayed that anyone who came to purchase a gun for the wrong reasons would not be able to do so.

Some time later, a very tough, rough looking, tattooed character approached the store. Through the store-front window, Robert saw that this man was accompanied by six or seven other equally tough-looking men on motorcycles parked in front. Immediately Robert had the sense that this man did not have good intentions. Standing by the gun counter, the man asked too many odd types of questions, so

Robert refused to sell any guns or ammunition to him and told him to leave. The man left in an angry huff, jumped on his bike, and motioned for the others to follow. Once outside, he made an obscene gesture through the window at Robert and pealed out of the parking lot with tires squealing and pipes roaring.

The next morning this same man returned with his gang plus a few more, but this time he didn't enter the store. The men simply began circling the store in the parking lot on their bikes. This, no doubt, was done with the intent of intimidating Robert or as a prelude to something worse. They kept up this harassment most of the day. They would drive out of the lot and return again in a few minutes to again circle and leave. All the while they would be looking through the front window at Robert.

Alone in the store, Robert prayed: "Lord, help me! Please send your angels to protect me and keep the store safe from harm."

After several hours of this harassment, the leather-jacketed gang drove out of the lot and never returned again.

Later, one of Robert's regular customers dropped by the store to visit. He mentioned that he'd been by earlier in the day but hadn't bothered to come in. Robert asked him why.

"Well, because the inside of your store was packed full of customers. I knew you'd be so busy you wouldn't have time to visit with me so I just left."

Yet...NO ONE was in the store at any time that day, except Robert!

Daniel answered, "O king, live forever! My God sent His angel, and he shut the mouths of the lions. They have not hurt me..." (Daniel 6:21).

FOOD FOR THOUGHT: Is it just another story of angelic protection or is it more than that? How often do we take for granted the fact that God is on our side and concerned about everything that concerns us?

"See, I am sending an angel ahead of you
to guard you along the way and to bring you
to the place I have prepared."
—*Exodus 23:20*

CHAPTER 26

Have I Experienced
An Angel Lately?

Yesterday, I was attending my regular Rotary Club meeting, in downtown Springfield, when an acquaintance, who is also a writer, asked me, "How is the writing going?"

To which I replied, "I'm writing to meet the next deadline, which is coming too quickly."

She answered with, "I'm into another project that needs to be written, but I just can't seem to get myself set down to write it. I don't have a handle on it and just can't seem to get up the energy to do this."

We talked further...one thing leading to another and then she asked me, "Now that you're working on your fourth angel book, how about you, have you had an angel encounter lately?"

I quickly shot back, "No, not that I can think of." The conversation then moved to travels we had taken and I said, "The latest was to Thailand in December..."

Immediately she broke in and asked, "When were you there and when did you leave?"

"We were there for a bit over two weeks and left on December 15, 2004." (The earthquake and resulting tsunami that devastated the area where we had been hit on December 25, 2004.)

She smiled, laughed, and said, "There's your own angel story!"

As I pondered that over our lunch, more things came to mind. I thought back to December 26, 2002. We were leaving Tulsa on I-44. It had snowed the previous day, but now the highways were clear with lots of snow on the shoulders and median. My wife Donna, son Kent, our dog Beethoven, and I were on our way home after celebrating Christmas with family in Tulsa. We were traveling in heavy traffic moving around 65 miles per hour. Suddenly a pick-up truck came sliding across the median directly at us. There was no room to avoid him by turning into the next lane. I stayed in our lane and prepared to take the blow of the pick-up bed as it skidded into our path.

It looked like a sure T-bone type collision, but at the last moment, his truck caught and spun out of my lane and just side-swiped us. Our car was totaled, but all of us, including Beethoven, escaped and walked away! I suffered a whip-lash injury, but otherwise we were well, just showered with shards of shattered glass. We were taken to the emergency of a nearby hospital for examination and treatment. The highway patrol officer on the scene told me, "It's an absolute miracle that you escaped injury or being hit by another car! The angels must have been riding with you."

Then in September and October of 2002, we had been in

Moscow teaching at the Moscow Theological Institute. While we were there, our Russian hosts took us down to the theatre district to take in the Bolshoi and to see a Russian production, a celebration of their ethnics. These were fabulous productions. We also took in a concert, all in the same district where ten days later the Chezchnians took over a downtown theatre and the loss of lives were in the hundreds. Another close escape!

Well...none of us actually saw an angel at work, but as my wife and I look back, we often praise the Lord for His protecting care! Were angels involved? I don't know, but to answer the question, they sure could have been, and we didn't recognize their protection.

FOOD FOR THOUGHT: I could say, along with Charlie Shedd, "These were moments when I felt the brush of angels' wings." Angels at work or not, it's still comforting to think that God has provided care and protection for believers. What about you? Do you recall incidents that might have been an angelic intervention in the normal course of your life? If the veil could be pulled back to allow us to see angels at work, I believe that we would be absolutely surprised at how often they have come to our rescue!

About the Author

ROBERT STRAND is the author of more than 60 books, and his "Moments To Give" series has sold more than three million copies. A consummate storyteller, Robert knows how to blend the emotional impact of true stories with practical insights from his many years of pastoral experience to produce breakthrough results. He and his wife, Donna, live in Springfield, Missouri.